Botanicals and Signs of the Zodiac

Combine healing herbs with your astrological sign to help you achieve new levels of well-being, vitality and spiritual connection

Botanicals and Signs of the Zodiac

Combine healing herbs with your astrological sign to help you achieve new levels of well-being, vitality and spiritual development

The author of this book does not diagnose or prescribe treatments for diseases or injuries. Although the information in this book is drawn from many traditional herbal sources, the author is mindful that each person is unique and complex. For this reason, the reader is advised to consult a qualified health care professional regarding the use of herbs.

ISBN-13: 978-1530271054
ISBN-10: 1530271053

A Note From Leilah

Astrology, the study of the planets, the stars and their relationship to one another and to us requires years to learn. Actually, one never stops learning, nor studying it. Astrology is both science and art. In ancient Egypt, astrologers and astronomers were highly regarded. They lived with the Pharaohs in the temples where their knowledge and understanding of astrology enabled them to predict future events – such as knowing when to expect flooding from the Nile. Their knowledge insured the safety of the people and was considered crucial for the survival of the Ancient Egyptians.

This booklet came about because I wanted to create a practical, day-to-day readily useable and understandable guide of astrology and herbs that can be used easily by all on a daily basis. I invite you to live this way and integrate this empowering work into your life. For example, when I wake up on a Tuesday morning I go to my closet and choose something red. This is the color for Tuesday. On Wednesday I choose green. If I have a headache or a digestive problem I make the appropriate tea that harmonizes with what is happening celestially. I realize you must always listen to your own innate inner wisdom. If you wake up on Tuesday feeling angry and "hot under the collar," you may want to choose another more calming color. I share this wisdom I have gathered through the years as my gift to you. I have tried to present it in a way that you, my readers, my friends, my customers and those brand new to this work, will have an opportunity to live with greater health, happiness and peace. I share here the research of many people I respect - my teachers, my favorite books, and other writings by writers, all whom share the most accurate of information. I have found that this knowledge varies greatly from source to source, which has made me realize that astrology is both a fascinating science as well as a wondrous healing art. Because not all astrologers agree on the same theories, I have taken their information, internalized it and finally presented it in the best, most useable way I consider possible.

Let's make a journey through the astrological seasons together. The information I share is what I feel is the most accurate and appropriate for me. I encourage you to make your own discoveries.

Table of Contents:

Introduction

The earliest known histories of medicine and health care throughout the world, record the link between astrology, the human body and herbs. During the Renaissance era it was standard practice for all physicians and herbalists to have an understanding about astrology and herbs to effectively practice medicine.

Today, we are able to blend these great traditions into a new model of herbalism; one that enables physicians, herbalists and healers to use herbs in a way that is deeply transforming and profoundly healing.

Nicholas Culpepper, a well-known herbalist in the 18th Century said: "Medicine without astrology is like a lamp without oil."

Astrological Teas

Leilah and Natalie have thoughtfully created unique and delicious astrological tea blends based on medical astrology. These may strengthen specific areas of the body or body systems, and may ease related discomfort or dis-ease. These medicinal teas are beautiful and tasty, as well as therapeutic. With the exception of the Gemini tea, they do not contain caffeine.

How to Prepare Astrological Teas

To make a cup of our Astrological Teas place one heaping teaspoon of herbal blend in a tea filter or tea infuser placed into a cup or tea-pot. Pour one cup freshly boiled water (do not heat water in the microwave oven) over the herbs and let this steep for approximately 20 minutes (except Gemini tea which should be steeped 3 minutes), then strain. Add a little honey if desired, and drink warm.

Suggestion on Dosage

How often can I drink my Astrological Tea?

The right dosage always depends on a person's metabolism, dietary habits, stress level and other differences. As a general rule, a large and robust person requires a greater dosage (3 – 6 cups a day) than a smaller and/or frail individual (one cup a day). A calm, laid back person can get away with less dosage than a more stressed, active, hyper person. Children require less; the following rule is often used: Divide the child's weight in pounds by 150 to give the approximate fraction of the adult dose. Example: A fifty-pound child will require 50/150 or 1/3 of the adult dose.

Colors, Gem Stones, Days of the Week

Astrology assigns specific colors to each sign of the zodiac. Are you drawn to certain colors? Do you dislike certain colors? Why? How do they make you feel? Color therapy is a recognized healing art and science that is used to rebalance the energetic field, or aura, affecting our health and well-being.

Gem Stones (Birthstones)

Astrology assigns specific gem stones to each sign of the zodiac. In many cultures the healing properties of gems have been used to treat physical, mental and spiritual disorders.

Days of the week

Astrology assigns a planet to each day of the week. Which day of the week do you like best? What kinds of situations dominate your least favorite days of the week?

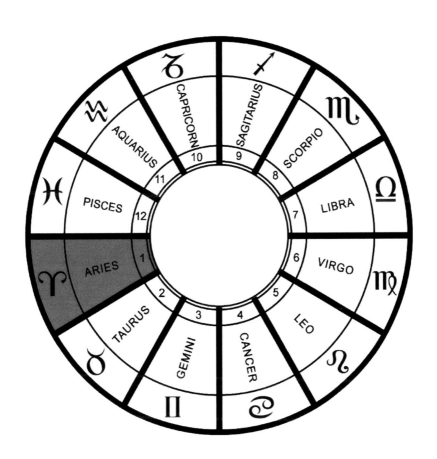

ARIES

"1 AM"

March 20ᵗʰ - April 19ᵗʰ Birthday People

If your birthday falls between March 20th and April 19th your astrological sign is Aries, the first house of the Zodiac. Additionally, if your astrological chart shows many planets in Aries, or if your Moon or Ascendant at the time of your birth is in Aries you may also want to balance possible Arian health conditions with herbs and natural remedies. Mars is the planetary ruler. It is the fiery planet. If you are not familiar with astrology you may want to contact an astrologer or go this website to find out about your birth chart: www.astro.com.

Those born in the sign of Aries have a tendency to have problems with the head, skull, brain, face (without the nose), and upper jaw. They may suffer from headaches and migraines, neuralgia, head injuries, toothache, eye problems, fevers, skin eruptions, poor memory, psychiatric disturbances, and vertigo. They should choose herbs and flower essences that calm their fiery nature and control their temper. Aries herbs are ruled by the planet Mars and their action is to move obstructions in the body, assist digestion, and increase memory. They are basil, blessed thistle, bloodroot, coriander, damiana, ginger, hawthorn, hops, horseradish, leeks, mustard, nettles, onion, peppers, peppermint, pine, skullcap, tarragon, tobacco, vitex, woodruff and yucca. Aries people are mentally driven. They need to balance their life with good nutrition and rest. They should avoid stressful situations, because irritation and agitation drains their energy.

13

Recipes To Balance Aries Tendencies:

Brain Tea

Prepare a cup of this tea blend to strengthen memory and improve concentration. Ginkgo stimulates cerebral circulation and oxygenation, Gotu Kola rejuvenates and revitalizes the nerves and brain, and Rosemary increases mental focus.

>1 cup Ginkgo
>1 cup Gotu Kola
>½ cup Rosemary

Tea for Strong Nerves

Prepare a cup of this tea blend and drink warm three times daily to strengthen the nervous system. Skullcap works on the central nervous system. It can rebuild nerve endings in the brain. Oat straw strengthens and nourishes the nervous system. It is used for nervous exhaustion, anxiety, and impaired sleep patterns. Oats contains calcium and magnesium, which are essential nutrients for the nervous tissues. It soothes the frayed feeling brought on by "burning the candle at both ends". St. John's Wort rebuilds a damaged nervous system and it can be used for neuralgia, agitation, anxiety and depression.

>1 cup Scullcap
>½ cup Oatstraw
>¼ cup St. John's Wort

Coffee Substitute

Aries people should avoid Coffee. Coffee is too stimulating and can irritate the nervous system, as well as affecting the brain in a negative way. Instead, drink a coffee substitute such as roasted Dandelion root, Chicory root, etc.

Vibrational Essences

Choose a vibrational essence, such as Negativity Releaser when you need to release tension, frustration, and anger. Tranquility of Mind is another essence for those whose thoughts bounce about a lot. This essence calms the mind and opens the 6th and 7th chakras.

Head Massage

Arians really need to take care of their head, in particular their brain. A daily head massage with Bhringaraj oil in the evening, before going to bed can calm the mind from excessive activity and promote sound sleep. Bhringaraj is an Ayurvedic herb known in India for its ability to also delay the aging process. Blend the following essential oils with Bhringaraj oil to quiet the mind.

> 1 tbsp Bhringaraj oil
> 15 drops Basil essential oil
> 5 drops Clary Sage

Astrological Tea Blend for Aries

Natalie and Leilah have formulated a delicious and health enhancing tea blend to bring balance to Arians.

- ♈ Raspberry Rooibos' decadent flavor stimulates the Arian's fiery nature.
- ♈ Skullcap brings mental balance to the head strong Arian.
- ♈ Feverfew calms the energized Arian.
- ♈ Oat Heads soothe the excited nerves of the Arian.
- ♈ Red Clover balances and nourishes the blood of the hot Arian character.
- ♈ Hibiscus sparks the taste buds of the curious Arian.
- ♈ Safflower and Pink Peppercorns add a lively nature, like the Arian, to this cup of tea.
- ♈ Goji Berries impart a fruity delight for the flaming personality of the Arian.

Colors, Gem Stones, Days of the Week

Mars is the fiery and bold planet that rules Aries. Its color is deep red, representing activity, aggression, passion, strength and power. If you are born in the sign of Aries and like the color red you have a strong and heated personality. If you get too obsessive about things, have a bad temper, or high blood pressure, use colors such as white or pink to tone down your Arians frayed nerves.

Red Coral corresponds to the planet Mars, which governs Aries. Red Coral strengthens the blood, improves energy and calms the emotions.

Tuesday is the day of the week ruled by the planet Mars. This is a good day for any type of laborious work, be it physical or mental. It is a high-energy day that will assist in finishing long-standing projects, and settling any issues with the authorities. Arians wear the color red on Tuesday to feel good.

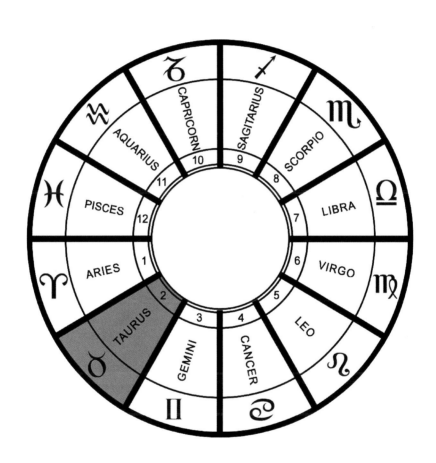

17

TAURUS

"I ENJOY"

April 20th - May 20nd
Birthday People

If your birthday falls between April 20th and May 20th your astrological sign is Taurus, the second house of the Zodiac. Additionally, if your astrological chart shows many planets in Taurus, or if your Moon or Ascendant at the time of your birth were in Taurus you may also want to balance possible Taurus health conditions with herbs and natural remedies. Venus, the love planet, is the planetary ruler. If you are not familiar with astrology you may want to contact an astrologer or go this website to find out about your birth chart: www.astro.com.

Taurus people have a tendency to have problems with their neck and throat. They may suffer from neck pain, sore throat, laryngitis, tonsillitis, torticollis, ear problems, respiratory problems, hyper- or hypo-thyroidism, and metabolic dysfunction, which may lead to weight problems. Taurean herbs are ruled by the planet Venus and bring emotional balance and gentle cleansing to the physical body of the headstrong Taurean. Choose herbs and vibrational essences for Taureans that help maintain optimal thyroid function, support digestion and metabolism, and keep the throat, respiratory and lymphatic systems clear: seaweeds, celery, chamomile, licorice, cardamom, coltsfoot, elder, lemon balm, licorice, marshmallow. mother-wort, mullein, oats, passionflower, raspberry, rose, rose geranium, spearmint, sugarcane, valerian, vanilla, vervein, vetivert, verbena, violets, willow, and yarrow. Taureans are lovers of the finer things in life such as good food and drink. They need to pay attention to their bodies and be physically active. They should avoid a sedentary life style as this can lead to obesity.

Recipes To Balance
Taurus Tendencies:

Lymphatic Cleanser Tea
Drink one cup three times daily to cleanse the lymphatic system.
>1 cup Cleavers
>1 cup Red Clover
>½ cup Calendula

Mucus Cleansing Tea
Prepare a cup of this tea blend and drink warm three times daily to liquefy and clear mucus from the body.
1 cup Licorice
½ cup Citrus peel
2 tbsp Thyme

Vibrational Essences
Taurus people enjoy comfort and luxury and must have security, especially financial security. Embracing Wealth will increase self-worth and self-esteem, allowing prosperity and abundance into your life. Inner Peace essence offers the gift of emotional inner peace and security, whenever the outer material world has failed to provide such. This essence relieves anxiety and restores optimism. People who seek fulfillment from the outside world, such as shop-aholics and gamblers, etc., will find fulfillment from an inner perspective of peace.

Seaweeds for the Thyroid
Seaweeds are excellent for a healthy thyroid. For example kelp can be used to replace chicken or beef stock. Simmer with liquids, at least 10 minutes and remove if desired, or leave it in for a richer broth. Taurus people should make sure to get an adequate amount of Sodium and Iodine for their health and well-being. Great sources of these minerals can

be found in many types of seaweed, such as kelp, dusle, bladderwrack, etc.

Neck Massage

A daily neck massage is important to the health and well-being of Taurus people. Use Keys to Heaven anointing oil before bed to prevent a morning stiff neck and to relax tight jaws. For swollen lymph nodes in the neck area or to relieve a sore throat take Lymph Drain drops. Additionally, make your own neck massage blend using Lymph Clear or the following oils:

> 1 tbsp Grape seed oil
> 15 drops Bay
> 10 drops Tangerine
> 5 drops Rose Geranium

Astrological Tea Blend for Taurus

Natalie and Leilah have formulated a delicious and health enhancing tea blend to bring balance to Taureans.

- ♉ Peach and Vanilla Rooibos's rich and decadent flavor is sure to please the palate of the dignified Taurean.
- ♉ Passion Flower relaxes the neck and jaw of the tense and strong-willed Taurean.
- ♉ Cleavers clears the lymphatic system of the overindulgent Taurean.
- ♉ Red clover's blood cleansing properties purifies the merry and extravagant Taurean's lifestyle.
- ♉ Oat Heads strengthens the nerves of the highly creative Taurean.
- ♉ Jasmine adds luxury and beauty for the life loving Taurean.
- ♉ Calendula imparts a stunning golden color for the luxury loving Taurean.
- ♉ Anise adds a tasty depth for the expressive and inquisitive Taurean.

Colors, Gem Stones, Days of the Week

Venus is the planet of love, relationships, beauty and money. It rules both Taurus and Libra. Pastel colors harmonize well with the sometimes introverted and reserved Taurean. If you are born in the sign of Taurus and like pastel and earthy colors you are calm, sensible, and deliberate. The color red negatively impacts Taureans and is best avoided to prevent them from seeing "red". If there are times you are looking to perk up your pastel colors, use the color black.

Diamonds, a girl's best friend, correspond to the planet Venus, which governs Taurus. Diamonds enhance creative abilities, beauty and charm. Substitute clear zircon for the more expensive diamond.

Friday is the day of the week ruled by the planet Venus. This day promises success, especially for women. Friendships blossom, happiness permeates the day, and life seems effortless. Taureans wear pastel colors on Friday to feel good.

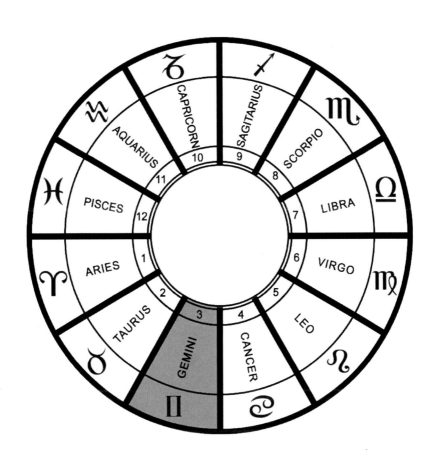

Gemini

♊

"I THINK"

May 21st - June 22nd
Birthday People

If your birthday falls between May 21st and June 22nd your astrological sign is Gemini, the third house of the Zodiac. Additionally, if your astrological chart shows many planets in Gemini, or if your Moon or Ascendant at the time of your birth were in Gemini you may also want to balance possible Gemini health conditions with herbs and natural remedies. Mercury is the planetary ruler, the communication planet. If you are not familiar with astrology you may want to contact an astrologer or go this website to find out about your birth chart: www.astro.com.

Geminis have a tendency to have problems with their arms and shoulders, the power of breath and the nervous system, including the brain. They may suffer from nervous disorders, neurological burnout, mental illness, depression, over stimulation of the mind, under eating, eczema, shoulder problems, carpal tunnel syndrome, asthma, bronchitis, and pneumonia. Choose herbs and vibrational essences for Gemini that calm their irritated nerves, balance overly analytical minds, and tonify their respiratory systems. Gemini herbs are ruled by the planet Mercury and their action is to alkalize the blood, support the nervous system and the respiratory system: almond, bergamot, brazil nut, celery, dill, fennel, fenugreek, filbert, flax, horehound, lavender, lemongrass, lemon verbena, marjoram, parsley, pecan, peppermint, pistachio, pomegranate.

At times, Geminis experience feelings of being on-edge, restlessness and anxiousness, and have difficulties stilling their minds. Insomnia and anxiety can bring on physical ailments; therefore, Geminis should control their nervous energy by engaging in activities that are calming, such as a soothing hobby, or working with their hands in some way.

Calming The Mind Tea

Prepare a cup of this tea blend and drink warm to calm the mind, and to balance left and right brain.

> 1 cup Tulsi
> 1 cup Gotu Kola
> ½ cup St. John's Wort

Sleepy Tea

Prepare a cup of this tea blend and drink warm before bedtime, to encourage deep and restful sleep.

> 1 cup Skullcap
> ½ cup Lemon Verbena
> ¼ cup Valerian

Lung Strengthening Tea

To strengthen the power of breath, as well as for any kind of respiratory issues, prepare this tea blend and drink three times daily:

> 1 cup Mullein leaf
> 1 cup Peppermint
> 5 drops Bergamot essential oil

Vibrational Essences

Choose vibrational essences to calm Gemini's highly intellectual mind to prevent restlessness and anxiety. Expand and deepen divine understanding with Meditation Release, or calm the mind and relax the body with Calm Grounding.

Meditation Blend

Although it may be difficult for Geminis to sit down and be still, they truly would benefit from daily meditations to quiet their mind. Use Peace in a Bottle anointing oil or make your own aromatherapy diffuser blend:

> 15 drops Lavender
> 15 drops Clary Sage
> 5 drops Vetivert

26

Astrological Tea Blend for Gemini People

Natalie and Leilah have formulated a delicious and health enhancing tea blend to bring balance to Geminians:

- ♊ Passion Fruit Green Tea stimulates intellectualism and gives energy for socialization to the mental Geminian.
- ♊ Coconut to allow flexibility and feed the nerves for the unpredictable Geminian.
- ♊ Jasmine creates a soothing nature to elicit patience to the restless Geminian.
- ♊ Almonds for alkalinity and to strengthen the nerves of the lively Geminian.
- ♊ Elder Berries to feed the immune system and bring balance to respiratory functions for the Geminian living in the fast lane.
- ♊ Lemongrass to encourage digestion and awaken personal power of the assertive Geminian.
- ♊ Ginger eases digestion and relieves inflammation for the eat-on-the-run Geminian.

Mercury is the planet of the mind and speech. It influences how we think and how we express ourselves, and rules Gemini, as well as Virgo. Green is their favorite color, as it represents growth and communication. If you are born in the sign of Gemini you are adventurous, creative, innovative, and you speak everyone's language. All shades of green will promote and enhance these activities. The color red can energize Geminians, but it can also create nervous energy and stress. If you need stability and direction, use the color black.

Emeralds correspond to the planet Mercury, which governs Gemini. Emeralds regulate the nervous system, calm the mind, improve speech, and soothe nerve pain. Emeralds strengthen the lungs and energize the breath, as well as increase flexibility of the mind and body. Substitute peridot or jade for the more expensive emerald.

Wednesday is the day of the week ruled by the planet Mercury. This is a good day for intellectual activities involving cerebral faculties, finance and banking. It is the perfect day for romance. Geminians, wear any shade of green on Wednesday to feel good.

Cancer

"1 FEEL"

June 23rd - July 23rd Birthday People

If your birthday falls between June 23rd and July 23rd your astrological sign is Cancer, the fourth house of the Zodiac. Additionally, if your astrological chart shows many planets in Cancer, or if your Moon or Ascendant at the time of your birth were in Cancer you may also want to balance possible Cancer health conditions with herbs and natural remedies. The Moon, the emotional planet, is the planetary ruler. If you are not familiar with astrology you may want to contact an astrologer or go this website to find out about your birth chart: www.astro.com.

Cancerians have a tendency to have problems with their digestion (especially from a weak stomach), breasts and reproductive systems. They may suffer from indigestion, eating disorders due to emotional imbalances, constipation, depression, brain chemistry imbalance, edema, breast problems (females), and sensitive teeth or gums. Choose herbs and vibrational essences for Cancerians to support the nervous system, balance their mood swings, strengthen the digestive system, and fortify the reproductive system. Cancer-herbs are ruled by the Moon. They promote action work with the subconscious mind, and for the emotions and instincts. They bring a higher degree of sensibility and help Cancerians flow with the rhythm of life. Moon herbs are: bladderwrack, buchu, cabbage, calamus, chickweed, club moss, coconut, cucumber, dulse, gardenia, grape, Irish moss, jasmine, lemon, lily, lotus, mallow, mesquite, myrrh, papaya, poppy, purslane, sandalwood, turnip, willow, and wintergreen. Cancerians feel very deeply, and the quality most needed is to balance their emotional ups and downs. Just as the Moon influences large bodies of water on earth, with high and low tides, so does the Moon affect the deep emotional feelings of the Cancerian.

Good Digestion Tea

Prepare a cup of this tea blend and drink warm before meals, or anytime during the day, to strengthen digestion.

1 cup Chamomile
1 cup Catnip
½ cup Spearmint

Keep The Bowels Moving Tea

To keep the bowels moving, Cancerians would benefit from this formula.

1 cup Peppermint
1 cup Red Clover
¼ cup Buckthorn

Woman's Balancing Tea

To strengthen the reproductive system, prepare this tea blend and drink three times daily.

1 cup Red Raspberry leaf
1 cup Lady's Mantle
¼ cup Rosemary

Vibrational Essences

Choose vibrational essences to bring emotional balance to the sensitive Cancerian. Mood Elevation is a "feel good" essence. When you feel better, you think clearer, and your thoughts are more connected to the world around you. Emotional Fortification re-enforces your emotional shield. It creates a tender protective screen that helps you come to terms with your emotional vulnerability. It will help you to feel more confident.

Breast Massage Oil

Use this oil topically during your self-breast exam, as well as to breathe in the balancing scents just prior to your exam.

2-3 Tbsp Evening Primrose oil
15 drops Fennel
5 drops Lemon
5 drops each of Clary Sage and Geranium

Astrological Tea Blend for Cancer People

The Herb Stop has formulated a delicious and health enhancing tea blend to bring balance to the Cancerian.

- ♋ Chocolate and Caramel Rooibos Tea comforts the highly empathic Cancerian.
- ♋ Jasmine soothes the emotions and hormones of the sensitive Cancerian.
- ♋ Pink Roses create a lifting feeling and bring in beauty to the idealistic and romantic Cancerian.
- ♋ Chrysanthemum, known as "gold flower" calms and soothes the highly emotional Cancerian.
- ♋ Eleuthero Root supports the emotions, hormones, and manages stress levels of the involved and instinctive Cancerian.
- ♋ Suma, known as "para todo" (for everything), is balancing and supportive to the whole body for the creative Cancerian...
- ♋ Rhodiola strengthens and shields the wise and intuitive Cancerian from harshness in the world.

Colors, Gem Stones, Days of the Week

The Moon is the heavenly body that influences our inner world, mind, emotions, and rules Cancer. White is the color that harmonizes well with the shy, withdrawn, sensitive and caring Cancerian. Its color is also light blue or sea-green. If you are born in the sign of Cancer and at times feel weak and have low energy, wear the color red. A cautionary note - this color does not harmonize well with Cancerians, and with prolonged use may undermine their sensitive and emotional nature.

Pearls are ruled by the Moon, which governs Cancer. Pearls can be worn to calm the emotions in the case of nervous excitability, as well as for restless sleep. Pearls increase bodily fluids, nourishing the bodily tissues and nerves. Pearls also strengthens the urinary system, and the female reproductive system

Monday is the day of the week ruled by the Moon. This is a good day for gardening, starting a new career, and for any kind of finance-related activities. Cancerians, wear white, light blue, or sea green on Mondays to feel good.

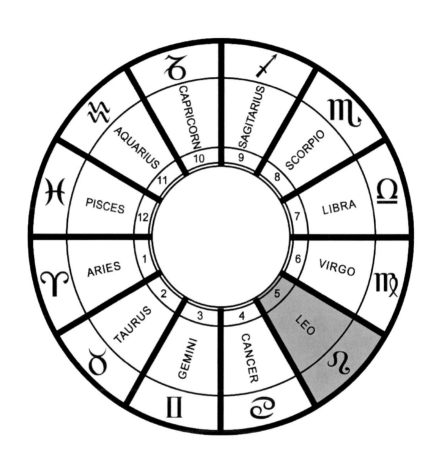

LEO

"I SHINE"

July 23ʳᵈ - August 23ʳᵈ
Birthday People

If your birthday falls between July 23ʳᵈ and August 23ʳᵈ your astrological sign is Leo, the fifth house of the Zodiac. Additionally, if your astrological chart shows many planets in Leo, or if your Moon or Ascendant at the time of your birth were in Leo you may also want to balance possible Leo health conditions with herbs and natural remedies. The Sun is the planetary ruler, the fiery planet. If you are not familiar with astrology you may want to contact an astrologer or go this website to find out about your birth chart: www.astro.com.

Leos have a tendency to have problems with the heart and arterial circulation. They may also have issues with their upper spine and back, lungs, as well as their eyes. They may suffer from heart conditions, high blood pressure, lower back problems, respiratory distress, and eye weakness. They should choose herbs and vibrational essences that strengthen the heart and eyes, equalize circulation, and relieve spasmodic afflictions. Leo herbs are ruled by the Sun and are good for those who have trouble with their self-image. Sun herbs build self-confidence and motivate one to complete one's goals. The Sun herbs are: angelica, bay, benzoin, carnation, cashew, cedar, celandine, centaury, chamomile, chicory, chrysanthemum, cinnamon, copal, eyebright, frankincense, ginseng, goldenseal, juniper, lime, lovage, marigold, mistletoe, oak, olive, orange, peony, pineapple, rosemary, saffron, St. John's wort, sesame, sunflower, tangerine, tea, walnut, witch hazel.

Leos are influenced by the Sun and therefore have a fiery nature. Keeping this fire in check is the key to their health and wellbeing. Just as the fire in a fireplace warms up a room on a cold winter night, the same fire if unchecked, can burn a house down. Leos need to practice breathing exercises to help them stay calm, increase oxygen and strengthen the lungs. Incidentally, solar flares affect Leos more than any other astrological sign.

Heart & Circulation Tea

Prepare a cup of this tasty tea blend and drink with lunch and before bedtime, to keep the heart and circulatory system healthy.

> 1 cup Hawthorn Leaf
> 1 cup Hawthorn Berry
> ¼ cup Pink Rose petals

Eye Strengthening Trail Mix

To strengthen the eyes, thoroughly chew one tbsp of this blend one to three times daily:

> 1 cup Bilberry berries
> 1 cup dried Blueberry berries
> ¼ cup Goji/Lycii berries

Eye Compresses

Rose hydrosol moisturizes dry and irritated eyes. Soak two cotton pads with rose hydrosol and cover eyes for about 20 minutes. This will cool the eyes, remove redness and burning sensation.

Strengthen The Eyes Massage Oil Blend

To strengthen the eyes massage a small amount of this blend around the eyes (NOT into the eyes) in the mornings and evenings.

> 5 drops Lemongrass
> 3 drops Cypress
> 2 drops Frankincense
> 1 tbsp Hazelnut oil

Back Massage Oil

Leos need regular back massages to strengthen the upper back and to loosen tight muscles. Mix 5 drops each of the following essential oils in 1 tbsp Sunflower oil:
Cypress, Rosemary, Juniper, Ginger, and Pink Grapefruit.

Vibrational Essences

Choose vibrational essences to bring self confidence to the noble Leo. Majestic Presence essence endows you with a sense of majestic presence, boosts inner confidence and brings out your positive ego. Confidence Builder essence has a positive effect under any circumstance that requires a greater feeling of confidence.

Astrological Tea Blend for Leo People

The Herb Stop has formulated a delicious and health enhancing tea blend to balance the inner fire of the Leo.

- ♌ Island Fruit Rooibos Tea is an explosion of flavor for the playful and fun loving Leo.
- ♌ Hawthorn brings balance and micronutrients to the heart of the lively Leo.
- ♌ Safflower's red color and circulatory properties motivates the powerful Leo.
- ♌ Osmanthus, an exotic and beautiful flower, purifies and enhances the skin of the beautiful and romantic Leo.
- ♌ Linden supports the circulatory system of the strong-willed Leo.
- ♌ Elder Flower enhances immunity, especially the respiratory system, for the expressive Leo.

The Sun is not a planet, but a star. This celestial body is the center of our solar system, all planets orbit around it, and it rules Leo. The Sun has a powerful influence on our personality and how we express ourselves outwardly. Gold and orange are the colors that harmonize well with the regal and charismatic Leo. If you are born in the sign of Leo, you express beautifully with radiance and confidence. Bright colors, such as yellow, orange, purple, and red are especially good for Leos. Colors that do not harmonize with the Leo are muted and pale colors.

Rubies are ruled by the Sun, which governs Leo. Rubies can be worn to strengthen the will, promote independence, increase confidence, as well as enhance personal power. It is the gem for Kings. Rubies strengthen the digestive system, heart, and circulation. Substitute Garnet for the more expensive Ruby.

Sunday is the day of the week ruled by the Sun. This is a good day for traveling and for entertaining friends. Leos, wear bright colors, red, orange, purple, or gold on Sunday to feel good.

August 24th - September 23rd Birthday People

If your birthday falls between August 24th and September 23rd your astrological sign is Virgo, the sixth house of the Zodiac. Additionally, if your astrological chart shows many planets in Virgo, or if your Moon or Ascendant at the time of your birth were in Virgo you may also want to balance possible Virgo health conditions with herbs and natural remedies. Mercury, the communication planet, is the planetary ruler. If you are not familiar with astrology you may want to contact an astrologer or go to this website to find out about your birth chart: www.astro.com.

Virgos have a tendency to have problems with the liver, solar plexus, the nervous system and the intestines. They may also have issues with the lungs, hips and the rectum. They may suffer from digestive and intestinal problems, hemorrhoids and rectal bleeding. Choose herbs and vibrational essences for Virgos that nourish the liver and bring it back to normal activity, soothe the nervous system, allay fear and heal the intestinal tract. Virgo herbs are ruled by Mercury and are good for those who are obsessive worriers leading to psychosomatic disorders. Mercury herbs support the digestive, nervous, and respiratory systems. Mercury herbs are: almond, bergamot, Brazil nut, caraway, celery, dill, elecampane, fennel, fenugreek, filbert, flax, horehound, lavender, lemongrass, lemon verbena, lily of the valley, marjoram, mulberry, parsley, pecan, peppermint, pistachio, pomegranate, summer savory.

Virgos have a finely tuned nervous system, which can make them very sensitive and intuitive. Mercury, Virgo's ruling planet, has dominion over the brain and the nervous system. This planet also controls the link between the mind and the functions of the body. Virgos have a tendency to worry themselves sick. They obsess over small details and find it hard to let things go. Virgos need good friends to talk to, to bounce off their problems, friends that help them see the bigger picture.

Just Let It Go Tea

Prepare a cup of this tasty tea blend and drink one to three cups anytime during the day, to help you let go of worry and anxiety.

1 cup Oatstraw
1 cup St. John's Wort
¼ cup Chamomile

Soothe The Stomach Tea

To calm a nervous stomach, or whenever you are worried about something, feeling anxious, prepare a cup of this tea. Sip this delicious beverage while writing down your worries into your "Worry Book". Then just close the book.

1 cup Catnip
1 cup Lemon Balm
1 cup Lemongrass
½ cup Spearmint

Mind Relaxation Oil Blend

Virgos can become irritable and critical of others when they are not feeling well. In this case, they need time to be alone and recuperate. The following essential oil blend creates a peaceful atmosphere, helping you quiet your mind and get centered again. Place a few drops into a diffuser while getting a massage, to facilitate meditation, while reading a good book, listing to relaxing music, or to help you quiet your mind.

9 drops Lavender
2 drops Lemon Balm
1 drop Vetivert

Vibrational Essences

Choose vibrational essences to calm the mind of the worrying Virgo. Clarity of Future essence will help you in times of worry, agony, anxiety and sleeplessness. Tranquility of Mind brings calmness and even sleepiness at times. This essence also calms the gastrointestinal system.

44

Astrological Tea Blend for Virgo People

Natalie and Leilah have formulated a delicious and health enhancing tea blend to balance the hard working Virgo.

- Citrus Rooibos Tea is an alkalizing and nutritive blend for nourishing the nervous system of the emotional Virgoan.
- Skullcap balances excessive thinking for the headstrong Virgoan.
- Marshmallow and Fennel soothe the delicate digestive system of the obsessively worried Virgoan.
- Milk Thistle supports the liver and gallbladder of the sensible and analytical Virgoan.
- Eleuthero and Oats strengthen the nerves and adrenals of the stressed and mentally oriented Virgoan.
- Lemongrass fortifies the solar plexus of the patient and inhibited Virgoan.

Mercury is the planet of the mind and communication. It influences how we think and how we express ourselves. It rules Virgo, as well as Gemini. Green is their favorite color, as it represents nature, growth and communication. If you are born in the sign of Virgo you have a quick mind that never misses a detail. You are a good listener, analytical, and strive to give your best advice. All shades of green, beige and brown are very soothing to the anxious Virgo. The color red can be too stimulating for Virgoans, and can also create anxiety, nervous energy and stress. If you need stability and direction, use earthy colors.

Emeralds correspond to the planet Mercury, which governs Virgo. Emeralds regulate the nervous system, calm the mind, improve speech, and soothe nerve pain. Emeralds strengthen the lungs and energize the breath, increase flexibility of the mind and body. Substitute peridot or jade for the more expensive emerald.

Wednesday is the day of the week ruled by the planet Mercury. This is a good day for intellectual activities involving cerebral faculties, finance and banking. It is the perfect day for gardening, especially planting trees. Virgoans wear earthy colors or any shade of green on Wednesday to feel good.

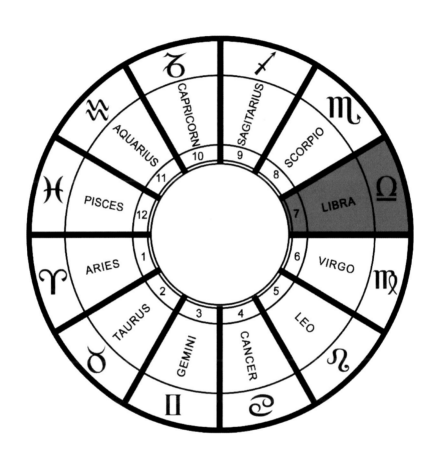

LIBRA

♎

"I BALANCE"

September 23rd - October 22nd Birthday People

If your birthday falls between September 23rd and October 22nd your astrological sign is Libra, the seventh house of the Zodiac. Additionally, if your astrological chart shows many planets in Libra, or if your Moon or Ascendant at the time of your birth were in Libra you may also want to balance possible Libra health conditions with herbs and natural remedies. Venus, the love planet, is the planetary ruler. If you are not familiar with astrology you may want to contact an astrologer or go to this website to find out about your birth chart: www.astro.com.

Libras have a tendency to have problems with the urinary system, the lower spine and the skin. They may also have issues in the lumbar region, buttock, and adrenal glands. Choose herbs and vibrational essences for Libras that support the urinary system, (kidneys, bladder, urethra), the lower back, and the skin. Libra herbs are ruled by Venus and are gently cleansing to keep a proper acid/alkaline balance. Too much acidity in the body can interfere with proper kidney function. Venus herbs are: alfalfa, apricot, birch, burdock, cardamom, cherry, cornflowers, cowslip, crocus, elder, feverfew, geranium, goldenrod, gooseberry, hibiscus, lady's mantle, lemon balm, licorice, mugwort, oats, orchid, passionflower, pea, peach, pear, periwinkle, plum, primrose, raspberry, rose, rose geranium, sagebrush, spearmint, strawberries, thyme, valerian, vanilla, vervain, vetivert, verbena, violets, willow, yarrow.

Libras are generally very healthy. They have a wonderful ability of being able to tolerate junk food for years without showing signs of ill health. Disregarding the laws of nature eventually can impair kidney function, making Libras susceptible to uric acid build up. The skin may also be affected, showing signs of acne, eruptions, and other skin problems. Balance in all things is the key to Libra's health and wellbeing.

Acid/Alkaline Balancing Tea

To maintain a proper acid/alkaline balance is particularly important for Libras. The following tea blend can be prepared and enjoyed three times a day and specifically before going to bed.

1 cup Chamomile
1 cup Peppermint
1 cup Lemon Peel

Healthy Kidney Tea

Libras need to drink plenty of water and healthy teas to flush out built-up waste and free their bodies of toxins. This nourishing herbal tea blend is effective in helping Libras maintain optimum urinary tract health.

1 cup Cornsilk
1 cup Nettle leaf
1 cup Rosehips
½ cup Spearmint

Lumbar Oil Blend

When Libras overexert themselves, they will notice it first in the lower back. Lower back massages with the following oil blend can be helpful to de-stress the lumbar area.

9 drops Ponderosa Pine
5 drops Lemon
1 drop Sweet Birch

Vibrational Essences

Choose vibrational essences to help Libras feel confidant when making choices. Choice Affirming essence has a grounding effect. It also has an impact on the heart chakric system, grounding and centering the emotions. It does not suppress them, it balances and centers them. Mentally, this essence re-enforces and stabilizes a stronger focus on what you want. It integrates body, mind and emotions.

50

Astrological Tea Blend for Libra People

Natalie and Leilah have formulated a delicious and health enhancing tea blend to balance the harmony-loving Libra.

- ♎ Chocolate Honeybush Tea & Cacao nibs are delicious for the healthy Libran that can afford to indulge.
- ♎ Banana Rooibos Tea & Bananas support healthy potassium and kidney balance to the Libran's "life of the party" personality.
- ♎ Cornsilk & Goldenrod soothes the urinary system for the balance seeking Libran.
- ♎ Nettle leaf creates equilibrium for the Libran through nutrition and elimination.
- ♎ Linden is a flavorful and heart warming tea for the loving and romantic Libran.
- ♎ Cornflowers are vibrant and lively for the social and active Libran.

Colors, Gem Stones, Days of the Week

Venus is the planet of love, relationships, beauty and money, and rules Libra, as well as Taurus. Pastel colors harmonize well with Libras, the sign of peace, harmony, and all that is aesthetic, beautiful and good. If you are born in the sign of Libra you like pastel and earthy colors, which keeps you balanced and grounded. Bright colors negatively impact Libras and are best avoided. If you are looking to perk up your pastel colors, you can use the colors black or dark blue.

Diamonds, a girl's best friend, correspond to the planet Venus, which governs Libra. Diamonds enhance creative abilities, beauty and charm. The color of Libra is transparent or translucent. Substitute clear zircon for the more expensive diamond.

Friday is the day of the week ruled by the planet Venus and this day promises success, especially for women. Friendships can blossom, happiness permeates the day, and life seems effortless. Libras, wear pastel colors on Friday to feel good.

SCORPIO
♏

"I DESIRE"

October 23rd - November 22nd Birthday People

If your birthday falls between October 23rd and November 22nd your astrological sign is Scorpio, the eighth house of the Zodiac. Additionally, if your astrological chart shows many planets in Scorpio, or if your Moon or Ascendant at the time of your birth were in Scorpio you may also want to balance possible Scorpio health conditions with herbs and natural remedies. Pluto is the planetary ruler, the transformational planet. If you are not familiar with astrology you may want to contact an astrologer or go to this website to find out about your birth chart: www.astro.com.

Scorpios have a tendency to have problems with their reproductive and urinary systems. They may also have issues with their glandular systems and sex organs. Scorpios are unable to rest and relax, and therefore, may also suffer from mental and physical exhaustion. Choose herbs and vibrational essences for Scorpios that support and rejuvenate the glandular, reproductive, and urinary system. Scorpio herbs support sexual drive and the desire to procreate. They also cleanse the body of toxins that may otherwise accumulate in the bladder and reproductive organs causing inflammatory disorders. Pluto herbs are: blessed thistle, leek, horseradish, wormwood, and sarsaparilla.

Scorpio rules the reproductive organs, the organs of regeneration and life-giving energy. An active sex life is essential to their health and wellbeing. Scorpios also need a healthy diet in order to keep up their energy and their positive outlook on life. If Scorpios experience emotional difficulties they become ill and may indulge in liquor. However, they do not handle alcohol well, since it is toxic to their system. Scorpio people have strong bodies and excellent recuperative powers. It has been said that Scorpios look old when they are young and young when they are old.

Prostate Tea

Scorpio men need to take care of their reproductive system, especially the prostate gland. The following tea blend can be prepared and enjoyed three times a day to prevent prostate problems.

> 1 cup Nettle root
> ½ cup Peppermint
> ¼ cup Ginger
> ¼ cup Saw Palmetto

Moon Cycle Tea

Scorpio women may benefit from drinking 1 – 3 cups daily of the following tea blend to promote a healthy reproductive system:

> 1 cup Red Raspberry
> 1 cup Damiana
> ½ cup Spearmint

Lover's Oil

Scorpios are the great lovers of all the astrological signs. The following oil blend supports their intense passion and hypnotic powers:

> 9 drops Ylang Ylang
> 5 drops Sandalwood
> 1 drop Clove

Vibrational Essences

Scorpios have a need to find a balance within their own spiritual nature, to stabilize the material world with the spiritual world. **Spiritual Expansion** essence attunes you to your own spiritual state of being, feeling more spiritual but also grounded in the physical world. **Spiritual Expansion** can help you with your meditations, and expand your mind. This essence may be beneficial for people who are searching and looking for answers in life, seeking to answer the question "WHY"; for searchers, explorers, adventurer, etc. **A HA! I've Got The Answer** is another essence that stimulates deep understanding and may perhaps bring forth an epiphany.

Astrological Tea Blend for Scorpio People

Natalie and Leilah have formulated a delicious and health enhancing tea blend to balance the mystifying and intense Scorpio.

- ♏ Cherry Rose Rooibos' sensual flavor feeds the desires of the Scorpian.
- ♏ Damiana's (Turnera aphrodesiaca) supports healthy sexual desire, reproductive health and urinary health for the magnetic and sexual Scorpian.
- ♏ Ashwagandha in Sanskrit means "vitality of the horse", known to increase desire, vitality and reproductive health as well as calming the mind for the mysterious Scorpian.
- ♏ Roses are a sensitive and hypnotic plant that brings up feelings of love and beauty for the perceptive Scorpian.
- ♏ Ginkgo's powerful and intense properties may be beneficial for mental focus and circulation to the extremities for the transformational and reactive Scorpian.
- ♏ Blessed Thistle has been used through history for oxygenation and to support liver health for the imaginative Scorpian.

Colors, Gem Stones, Days of the Week

Pluto is the planet of major transformation, power and control, leadership, and self-mastery. It rules Scorpio. Rich and mystical colors, deep purple and scarlet red, captivate the intense and unpredictable kaleidoscope of Scorpio. If you are born in the sign of Scorpio, you like all colors that have a hint of mystery. This balances your intense moods and ever-changing states of mind. Pale and pastel colors do not harmonize well with the diverse and secretive Scorpio. Pick any color to reflect your moods, and states of mind.

Rubies, as well as bloodstone, harmonize well with the planet Pluto, which governs Scorpio. Ruby is considered the most powerful gem. It enhances both vitality and vigor. Substitute garnet for the more expensive ruby.

Tuesday is the day of the week ruled by the planet Mars and Pluto. This is a good day for any type of laborious work, be it physical or mental. It is a high -energy day and assists in finishing long-standing projects, settling any issues with the authorities. Scorpios, wear the color red on Tuesday to feel good.

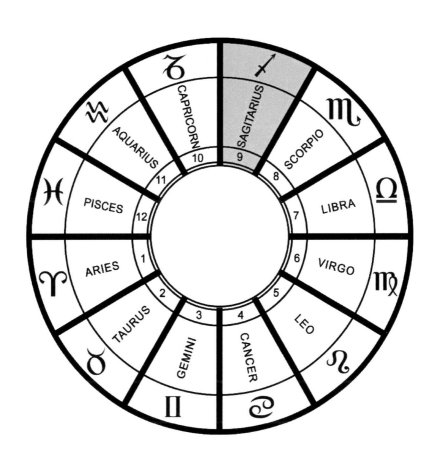

SAGITTARIUS

"I EXPLORE"

November 23rd - December 21st Birthday People

If your birthday falls between November 23rd and December 21st your astrological sign is Sagittarius, the ninth house of the Zodiac. Additionally, if your astrological chart shows many planets in Sagittarius, or if your Moon or Ascendant at the time of your birth were in Sagittarius you may also want to balance possible Sagittarius health conditions with herbs and natural remedies. Jupiter is the planetary ruler, the planet of expansion. If you are not familiar with astrology you may want to contact an astrologer or go to this website to find out about your birth chart: www.astro.com.

Sagittarians have a tendency to have problems with the hips, thighs and the sacral region of the spine. They may also have issues with the liver. Sagittarians spark into immediate and quick action when needed and may at times burn the candle at both ends. Choose herbs and vibrational essences for Sagittarians that support and rejuvenate the liver. Sagittarian herbs are ruled by the planet Jupiter. Their action is to cool and cleanse the blood, reduce fever and heal. They also strengthen the lower part of the body, and the nervous system. Jupiter herbs are: anise, borage, chestnut, cinquefoil, clove, dandelion, endive, fig, honeysuckle, horse chestnut, hyssop, linden, liverwort, maple, meadowsweet, nutmeg, sage, sarsaparilla, sassafras, star anise, wood betony, and yellow dock.

Sagittarians have an active and sensitive liver. Their health may be at stake if they eat too many fatty foods or too many carbohydrates. Their liver suffers instantly from overuse of alcohol. To keep up their high energy levels, Sagittarians need to exercise in fresh air, especially leg exercises, such as walking. Jupiter also rules the pituitary gland, which is the master gland that regulates hormone production and physical growth. The Sagittarian's mascot reveals a half human and half horse, symbolizing the union of mind and body.

Blood and Liver Cleansing Tea

To support the Sagittarian's sensitive liver prepare the following tea blend and drink with meals.

1 cup Red Clover
½ cup Dandelion leaf
¼ cup Schizandra

Before Work-Out Power Shake

Sagittarians are great athletes and love playing sports. To improve athletic performance and endurance enjoy a power shake one to two hours before any physical work-out. Mix the following ingredients together and get powered-up:

1 cup Green Juice
½ tsp Rhodiola
½ tsp Maral
½ tsp Maca

Jet Lag Oil

Sagittarians love traveling, especially foreign travels. Jet lag may be a setback to the adventurous and high spirited Sagittarian. Use Peppermint and Eucalyptus before your journey and Lavender and Rose Geranium, or the following blend to calm upon arrival.

9 drops St. John's Wort
5 drops Sandalwood
3 drop Lavender

Vibrational Essences

Sagittarians are always on-the-go and may sometimes suffer from burn-out and low energy levels. Re-Capturing Control essence builds momentum and helps them get back on track again. Another essence, Stamina and Will Enhancement, is excellent for the athletic Sagittarian; it gives a boost of energy without steroids, but more than that, a boost of will. Very often it is the will that increases ones potential.

Astrological Tea Blend for Sagittarian People

The Herb Stop has formulated a delicious and health enhancing tea blend to balance Sagittarians.

- Coffee flavored Rooibos has a tasteful flavor without stimulating the adventurous and inspiring Sagittarian.
- Vanilla Honeybush soothes the senses of the volatile and fiery Sagittarian.
- Rhodiola gives strengths and stamina to support the outgoing nature of the athletic Sagittarian.
- Fo-Ti, known as the Oriental "Elixir of Life", is rejuvenating and liver supporting to the quickly emoting, yet wise Sagittarian.
- Ginkgo increases mental alertness and open-mindedness of the highly intelligent and honest Sagittarian.
- Honeysuckle cools the blood of the passionate and on-the-go Sagittarian.
- Feverfew soothes inflammation of the active, outdoorsy Sagittarian, and calms the mind of the sometimes tactless and unfeeling Sagittarian.
- Cornflower imparts a graceful nature and calming influence to the highly likeable Sagittarian.

Jupiter is the planet of expansion, growth, and good-fortune. It rules Sagittarius. The colors yellow and blue are the best colors for the adventurous, independent and freedom-loving Sagittarian. If you are born in the sign of Sagittarius, you like clean and pure colors, and at times you like white, to soothe and relax you. The color black does not have a positive influence on the Sagittarian and is best avoided. Red increases joie de vivre and sets off a "get-up-and-go" attitude.

Yellow sapphire gives energy and vitality. This gem stone harmonizes well with Jupiter, which governs Sagittarius. Yellow sapphire strengthens the nervous system and the intellect and gives Sagittarians positive mental energy. Substitute citrine for the more expensive yellow sapphire.

Thursday is the day of the week ruled by the planet Jupiter. This is a good day to show reverence and to offer gratitude and compensation to our teachers and all people we learn or gain knowledge from. It is a good day for spiritual practices and to receive divine blessings. Sagittarians, wear the color yellow or blue on Thursday to feel good.

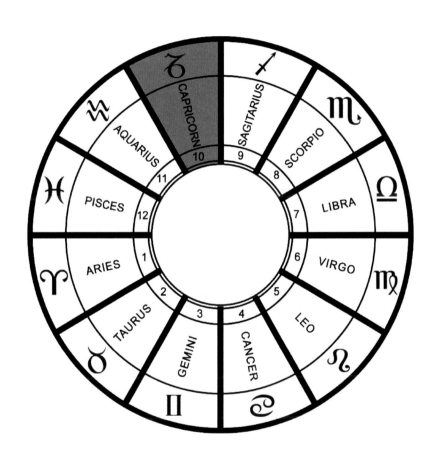

CAPRICORN

♑

"1 ACHIVE"

December 22nd - January 19th Birthday People

If your birthday falls between December 22nd and January 19th your astrological sign is Capricorn, the tenth house of the Zodiac. Additionally, if your astrological chart shows many planets in Capricorn, or if your Moon or Ascendant at the time of your birth were in Capricorn you may also want to balance possible Capricorn health conditions with herbs and natural remedies. Saturn is the planetary ruler, the task maker planet. If you are not familiar with astrology you may want to contact an astrologer or go this website to find out about your birth chart: www.astro.com.

Capricorns have a tendency to have problems with their skeletal structure, joints, knees, teeth and the skin. They are prone to diseases, disorders, and injuries to the legs, knees, and bones. Choose herbs and vibrational essences for Capricorns that strengthen the bones, loosen stiff joints, and maintain healthy teeth. Capricorn herbs are ruled by the planet Saturn and are high in minerals to help maintain a strong physical structure: amaranth, beet, belladonna, boneset, buckthorn, comfrey, cypress, elm, horsetail, lobelia, mullein, pansy, patchouli, poplar, quince, skullcap, slippery elm, Solomon's seal, tamarind.

Capricorns strive for social status and recognition, success in business or career. They are driven individuals. Honest, stable, and hardworking, they thoroughly explore all possibilities before deciding on a "safe" course. They tend to do things in excess, overwork, skip meals, and then eat too much at one time. They should go easy with spicy foods, because these may cause intestinal upsets. Worrying drains their energy and spirit. At times, Capricorn's surprising mood swings earn the adjective – "capricious". Capricorns are known for their longevity. Their health gets better as they get older.

High-Mineral Tea

Prepare a warm cup of this tasty tea blend and drink with meals or anytime in-between, to strengthen bones and teeth.

> 1 cup Horsetail
> 1 cup Alfalfa
> 1 cup Lemon Verbena

Castor Oil Packs

Since Capricorns have a tendency to experience problems with their joints, they may find relief by applying Castor oil packs on painful areas to relieve pain and swelling.

Meditation Oil Blend

Although Capricorns are practical and rational, regular meditations can help them gather inner strength to control deeply suppressed emotions. Place 5 drops into a diffuser before meditation to enhance meditations:

> 5 drops Sandalwood
> 3 drops Ho-Wood
> 3 drops Tangerine

Teeth and Gum Powder

Keep that beautiful smile, Capricornians! Strengthen your teeth and gums with the following tooth powder:

> 1 tbsp Baking Soda
> 1 tbsp Horsetail powder
> 1 tbsp Lemon peel powder

Place a small amount of tooth power on a tooth brush and brush for several minutes once a day. Go gently at first, to avoid bleeding gums.

Vibrational Essences

The highly active and driven Capricorn deserves some down time, to relax the body and release inner tension. Evening Relaxation essence encourages deep relaxation to allow them to reconnect again on a deep core level. In spite of their naturally logical and skeptical side, Capricorns show an interest in mysticism. Tranquility of Mind essence is relaxing and connects the practical Capricorn with the infinite intelligence. It is truly a key to wisdom!

Astrological Tea Blend for Capricorn People

Natalie and Leilah have formulated a delicious and health enhancing tea blend for the independent and hardworking Capricornian.

- ♑ Marzipan Rooibos Tea is mild, balancing and uplifting for the highly driven Capricornian.
- ♑ Lemon Chiffon Rooibos Tea is clearing and inspiring to the steadfast and head-strong Capricornian.
- ♑ Shavegrass brings strength and power to the enterprising and ambitious Capricornian.
- ♑ Boneset as its name suggests supports and strengthens the physical structure of the stable and tough Capricornian.
- ♑ Lobelia calms and relaxes the body of the stubborn and capricious Capricornian.
- ♑ Schisandra berries support liver function for the sometimes emotionally suppressive, yet loving Capricornian.

Colors, Gem Stones, Days of the Week

Saturn is the planet of karma, work, discipline and responsibility, and rules Capricorn. The colors dark blue and black are the best colors for the practical, prudent, ambitious Capricornian. If you are born in the sign of Capricorn you like dark and plain colors, especially earthy colors, to balance your moods and help you stay connected to earthly matters. The color red does not have a positive influence on the Capricornian and is best avoided, as it may bring out negative traits. Capricornians do not like the color yellow. Black and white combinations are some of their all time favorite colors.

Blue sapphire helps calm the nerves and emotions, this gem stone harmonizes well with Saturn, which governs Capricorn. Blue sapphire promotes calm, peace, and detachment, and bestows Capricornians with good health and longevity. Substitute amethyst for the more expensive blue sapphire.

Saturday is the day of the week ruled by the planet Saturn. This is a good day to fast and undertake play activities. Do not indulge in any type of luxury. Saturday is the day where big success can be achieved, especially during the first half of the day (morning). It is also a good day for working with the earth. If, on Saturday, all your efforts are being launched to resolve legal problems, chances are the problems will be resolved once and for all. Capricornians wear the color dark blue or black on Saturday to feel good.

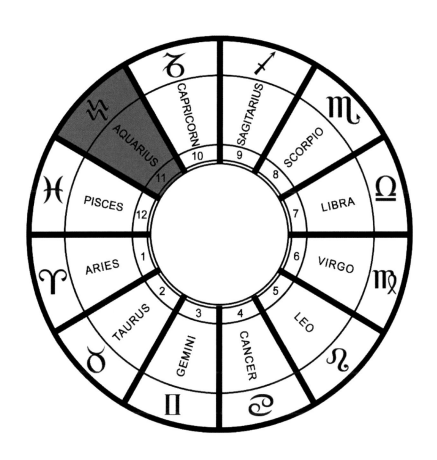

AQUARIUS

♒

"I INVENT"

January 20th - February 18th Birthday People

If your birthday falls between January 20th and February 18th your astrological sign is Aquarius, the eleventh house of the Zodiac. Additionally, if your astrological chart shows many planets in Aquarius, or if your Moon or Ascendant at the time of your birth were in Aquarius you may also want to balance possible Aquarian health conditions with herbs and natural remedies. Uranus is the planetary ruler, the rebellious planet. If you are not familiar with astrology you may want to contact an astrologer or go this website to find out about your birth chart: www.astro.com.

Aquarians have a tendency to have problems with their calves, ankles (organs of locomotion), the blood (anemia) and blood stream, the nervous system, many areas of the brain, and nerve impulses. Restrictions, in any form, are irritating to the Aquarian. Yet, paradoxically as it may seem, inwardly they crave discipline. They should avoid coffee or any kind of caffeinated foods and drinks, as these can make them nervous and jittery, which may affect their sleep patterns. Aquarians have an extremely sensitive mind. Lack of sleep can easily throw them off balance, leaving them with a feeling of overload and of being overwhelmed. The herbs for Aquarius are valerian and lady's slipper, nervines, herbs for emotional stress, anxiety and insomnia. These are also excellent for muscle cramps, nervous system, pain, spasms, and ulcers. Here are some herbal tea recipes you can prepare yourself, and other ideas to bring balance to the Aquarian person.

To Strengthen the Nervous System

Prepare this tea blend and drink several cups a day during and after stressful times to support and strengthen the nervous system.

> 1 cup Oat straw
> 1 cup St. John's Wort
> ½ cup Skullcap

Insomnia

Prepare a cup of this tea blend and drink warm one hour before bed to induce sleep.

> 1 cup Passionflower
> ½ cup Lavender
> ¼ cup Valerian

Emotional Stress and Anxiety

Prepare a cup of this tea blend during an emotional crisis, for anxiety or panic attacks. It has a calming effect, helping you regain emotional balance.

> 1 cup Lemon balm
> 1 cup Chamomile
> ½ cup Anise
> ¼ cup Valerian

Muscle Spasm and Pain

Prepare this tea when muscles are tight and painful. For a total relaxing experience sip it slowly while soaking in an Epsom salt bath.

> 1 cup Peppermint
> ½ cup Crampbark
> ¼ cup Valerian

Ulcers

Prepare this tea blend and drink warm, several cups a day, or whenever you suspect your ulcers acting up. This tea blend has a calming and soothing effect upon ulcers.

> 1 cup Marshmallow
> 1 cup Fennel
> 1 cup Licorice

Anemia

Floradix makes an excellent herbal extract to combat anemia. Nettle leaf, Dong Quai, and Red Raspberry.

Vibrational Essences

Choose vibrational essences that bring inspiration, as well as an ability to follow one's feelings in trying new endeavors, or when one's thinking is stuck. Combine **Stamina and Will Enhancement** with **Interest Expansion** and **Mental Motivation**, and take 3 drops 3 times daily.

Leg & Foot Massage

Leg and foot massages are ideal for Aquarian people. Use **Free the Soul** anointing oil or make your own blend:

> 1 tbsp Almond oil
> 15 drops Lavender essential oil
> 15 drops Roman Chamomile
> 5 drops Ponderosa Pine

Astrological Tea Blend for Aquarius

The Herb Stop has formulated a delicious and health enhancing tea blend to bring balance to Aquarians.

- Chocolate & Hazelnut Honeybush's decadent flavor inspires the Aquarian in you.
- Lemon Balm soothes the nerves of the busy Aquarian.
- Lavender calms the rebel in the Aquarian.
- Star Anise inspires the Aquarian to change the world.
- Valerian keeps the innovative Aquarian's feet firmly planted on the ground.
- Cacao Nibs satisfies the indulgent Aquarian.
- Malva's beautiful color stirs the thoughts of the Aquarian.
- Oat Heads builds the nerves of the busy Aquarian.

Colors, Gem Stones, Days of the Week

Uranus is the planet of change, surprise, awakening, and rebellion. It rules Aquarius. Psychedelic colors appeal to the imaginative, psychically intuitive, and "ahead of his time" Aquarian. If you are born in the sign of Aquarius you like a variety of colors ranging from the stark and bold to all the electric colors that change with light. The new generation colors are Aquarian colors, as they may make heads turn. This points to the truth that the Aquarian is ahead of his time. You like colors that are not conventional, with outlandish mixtures and patterns of two and more colors. Black is your all-time favorite and makes the Aquarian happy.

Aquamarine is the stone for the visionary Aquarians who are fighting for a better world. This gemstone urges you to seek freedom and independence and helps you to express your uniqueness. It also encourages the Aquarian to always question limiting beliefs with an open mind and to be willing to grow beyond them. Aquamarine promotes clear verbal expression. It aligns all the chakras and enhances the auric field for the risk-taking and courageous Aquarian.

Wednesday is the day of the week ruled by the planet Mercury and the higher octave Uranus. Uranus is an outer planet and some astrologers say it rules the nights, influencing the inner planets. Wednesday is a good day for intellectual activities involving cerebral faculties, finance and banking. It is the perfect day for romance. Aquarians, wear violet on Wednesday to feel good.

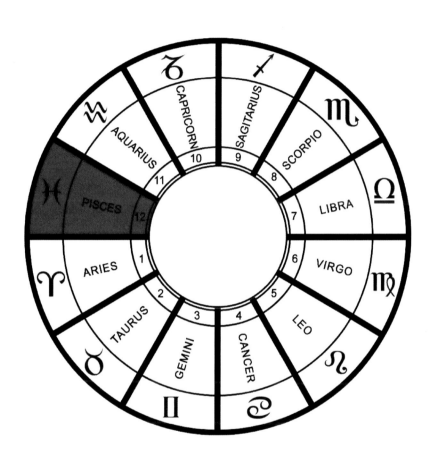

PISCES
♓

"I DREAM"

February 19ᵗʰ - March 19ᵗʰ Birthday People

If your birthday falls between February 19ᵗʰ and March 19ᵗʰ your astrological sign is Pisces, the twelfth house of the Zodiac. Additionally, if your astrological chart shows many planets in Pisces, or if your Moon or Ascendant at the time of your birth were in Pisces you may also want to balance possible Piscean health conditions with herbs and natural remedies. Neptune is the planetary ruler, the mystical planet. If you are not familiar with astrology you may want to contact an astrologer or go this website to find out about your birth chart: www.astro.com.

Pisces people have a tendency to have problems with their feet, toes and fluids of the body. The herbs for Pisces work with the kidneys and lymphatic systems, which pass fluids within the body, the spinal canal and the parathyroid. Choose herbs and flower essences for Pisces that open the mind to a greater sense of vision, as well as the ability to dream, both when asleep and awake. These herbs should enhance astral travel, but they may only be used as a key to learning: wild lettuce, lobelia, lotus, mugwort, willow, and the essence of yerba mansa. Irish moss is the main herb for Pisces, as it treats respiratory and intestinal disorders. Irish moss is rich in electrolyte minerals – calcium, magnesium, sodium and potassium, as well as mucilaginous compounds that assist the body with detoxification, boosting metabolism, strengthening the hair, skin and nails. If used persistently, Irish moss relieves every Piscean complaint.

Dream Tea
Prepare a cup of this tea blend and drink warm one hour before bed to induce prophetic dreams.
> 1 cup Mugwort
> 1 cup Lavender
> ½ cup Oatstraw

Lymphatic Tea

Prepare a cup of this tea blend and drink warm three times daily to relieve a congested lymphatic system.

> 1 cup Cleavers
> ½ cup Mullein
> ¼ cup Calendula

Blood Cleansing Tea

Piscean people enjoy a good life and like to indulge in food and drinks. For these reasons they are subject to gout, skin problems, swollen feet, mucous discharges, and other conditions due to toxic blood. Prepare a cup of this tea blend when symptoms occur, or to prevent them.

> 1 cup Red Clover
> 1 cup Lemongrass
> ¼ cup Juniper

Vibrational Essences

Choose vibrational essences when you need to retreat from worldly stress and housework. Expand your consciousness and allow yourself to dream with **Spiritual Expansion**, **Meditation Release**, or **Tranquil Calmness**. Take 3 drops 3 times daily.

Reflexology Foot Massage

Foot massages are ideal for Piscean people. Use White Light anointing oil or make your own massage blend:

> 1 tbsp Almond oil
> 15 drops Peppermint essential oil
> 15 drops Lavender
> 5 drops Blood Orange

Essential Oil Blend for Grounding

Use this essential oil blend in an aromatherapy diffuser, or blend with Grape Seed Oil for massage.

> 15 drops Lavender
> 10 drops Clary Sage
> 2 drops Vetivert

Astrological Tea Blend for Pisces

Natalie and Leilah have formulated a delicious and health enhancing tea blend to bring balance to Pisceans.

- ♓ Blueberry Rooibos and Vanilla Honeybush indulges the Piscean's decadent palate.
- ♓ Cleavers helps to restore the lymphatic flow to the Piscean.
- ♓ Dandelion Leaf manages the water balance of the swimming Piscean fish.
- ♓ Lavender saturates the mystical needs of the Piscean.
- ♓ Blue Violet brings the Piscean into their magical and creative world.
- ♓ Safflower purifies the indulgent behavior of the Piscean.

Colors, Gem Stones, Days of the Week

Neptune is the planet that influences the subconscious mind, dreams hopes, imagination, and the connection to spirituality. It is the planet that rules Pisces. Yellow is a happy color that uplifts the sensitive, gentle, intuitive, and sometimes withdrawn Piscean. If you are born in the sign of Pisces you like pale pastel colors, especially pale yellow, pale blue-green, violet, and white. The sensitive and evolved Piscean does not like bright or stark colors.

Amethyst is the gem for the sensitive Piscean. It can bring inner peace and calmness, as well as heighten intuition. It also repels negativity and attracts positive energy. Amethysts assist with healing, spiritual growth, and enlightenment.

Thursday is the day of the week ruled by the planet Jupiter and higher octave Neptune. Neptune is an outer planet and some astrologers say it rules the night, influencing the inner planets. Thursday is a good day to show reverence and to offer gratitude and compensation to our teachers and all the people we learn or gain knowledge from. It is a good day for spiritual practices and to receive divine blessings. Pisceans wear the color pale yellow or violet on Thursday to feel good.

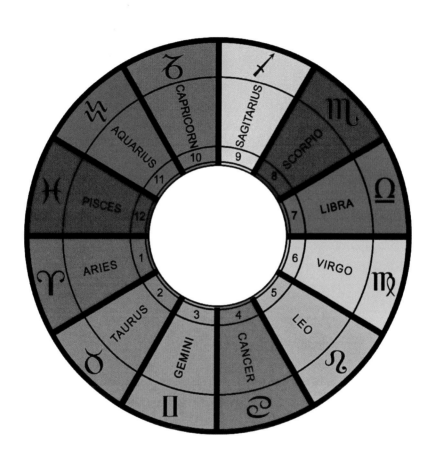

References

Frawley, Dr. David O.M.D. *Ayurvedic Healing.* Passage Press. 1989.

Bunker, Dusty. *Numerology and Your Future.* Schiffer Publishing. 1997

Toye, Lori. Loritoye.com. IAMAMERICA.com .

Astrogle.com

Sources

The Herb Stop
This is a place where you can find the Astrological Teas mentioned in this book, as well as essential oils, herbal extracts/tinctures, herbal capsules, and much more.
www.HerbStopOnline.com

Astro.com
This can help you figure out your Natal Chart, Ascendant, and more.

Made in the USA
Las Vegas, NV
04 May 2025

21607399R00052